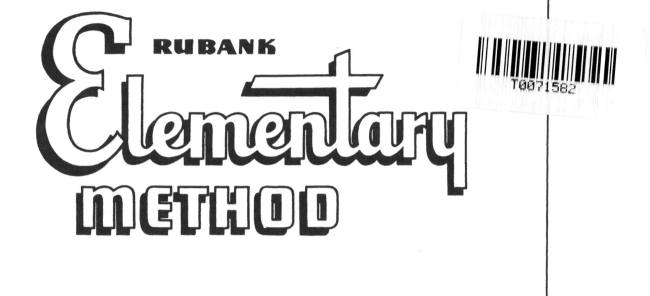

RUBANK Elementary METHOD

DRUMS

PAUL YODER

A FUNDAMENTAL COURSE FOR INDIVIDUAL
OR LIKE-INSTRUMENT CLASS INSTRUCTION

RUBANK®

HAL•LEONARD®
CORPORATION
7777 W. BLUEMOUND RD. P.O. BOX 13819 MILWAUKEE, WI 53213

Holding the Sticks

The snare drum sticks should be held as shown in the two sketches below.

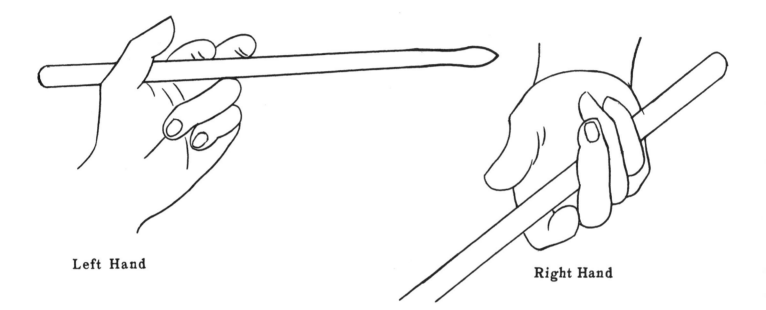

Left Hand

Right Hand

The Long Roll

The most important fundamental in all drumming is the long roll. It is made with alternating double strokes of each hand in the following manner and may be started with either stick. As an exercise this roll should be started very slowly and gradually speeded up to the limit of the performer's ability, then just as gradually slowed down to the starting point.

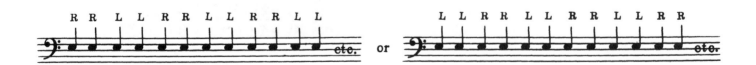

The second stroke of the double stroke in each case should be a bounce rather than a separate stroke. Only in this way can the real closed roll be attained. This exercise should be practiced daily.

Rubank Elem. Meth. for Drums 39

Table of Time Values

The drummer should learn the system of counting time as outlined here and count aloud whenever practicing.

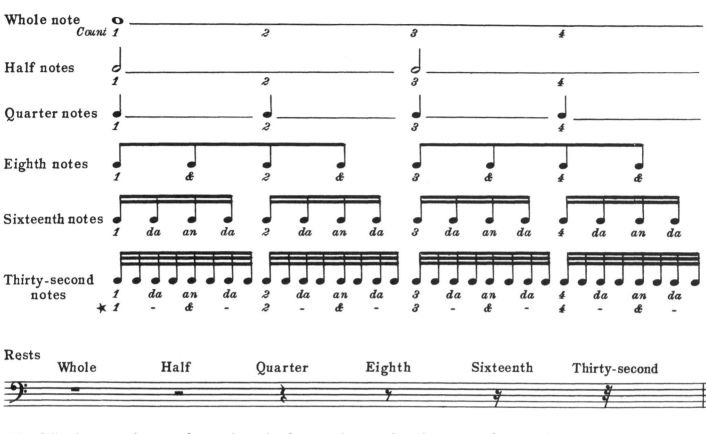

Rests

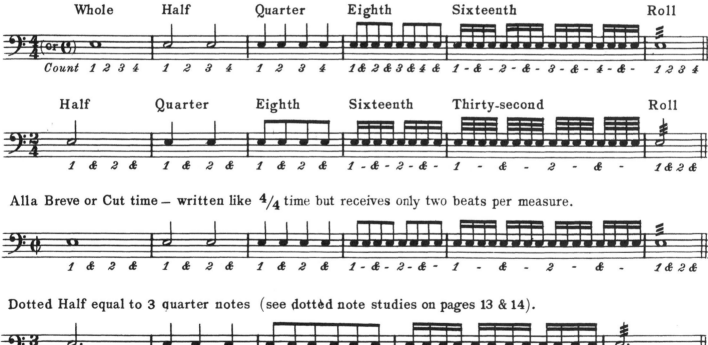

The following exercises are for study and reference in counting time — not for practice.

Alla Breve or Cut time — written like 4/4 time but receives only two beats per measure.

Dotted Half equal to 3 quarter notes (see dotted note studies on pages 13 & 14).

Dotted Quarters equal to 3 eighth notes (see pages 13 & 14).

✶ For convenience in writing these symbols will be used to designate the proper count.

Studies for Snare Drum

The sticking is marked above each line. This is recommended but must not be considered obligatory. A drummer should be able to start any passage with either hand. The count below each line should be spoken aloud while practicing, this is very important.

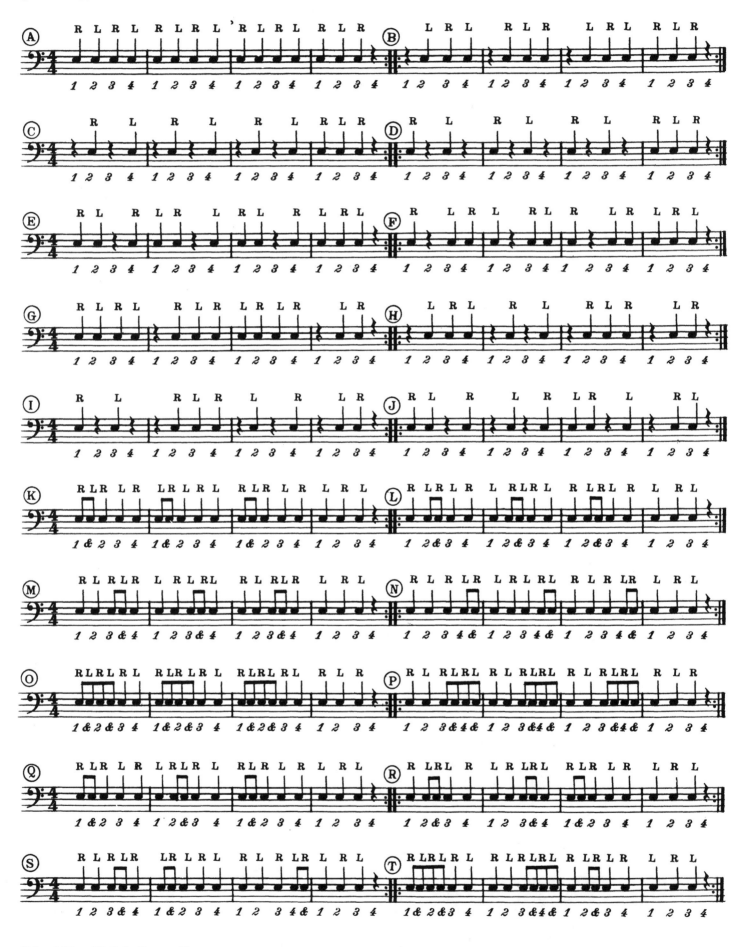

Alla Breve or Cut time (¢) is written like $^4/_4$ time but receives only two beats per measure.

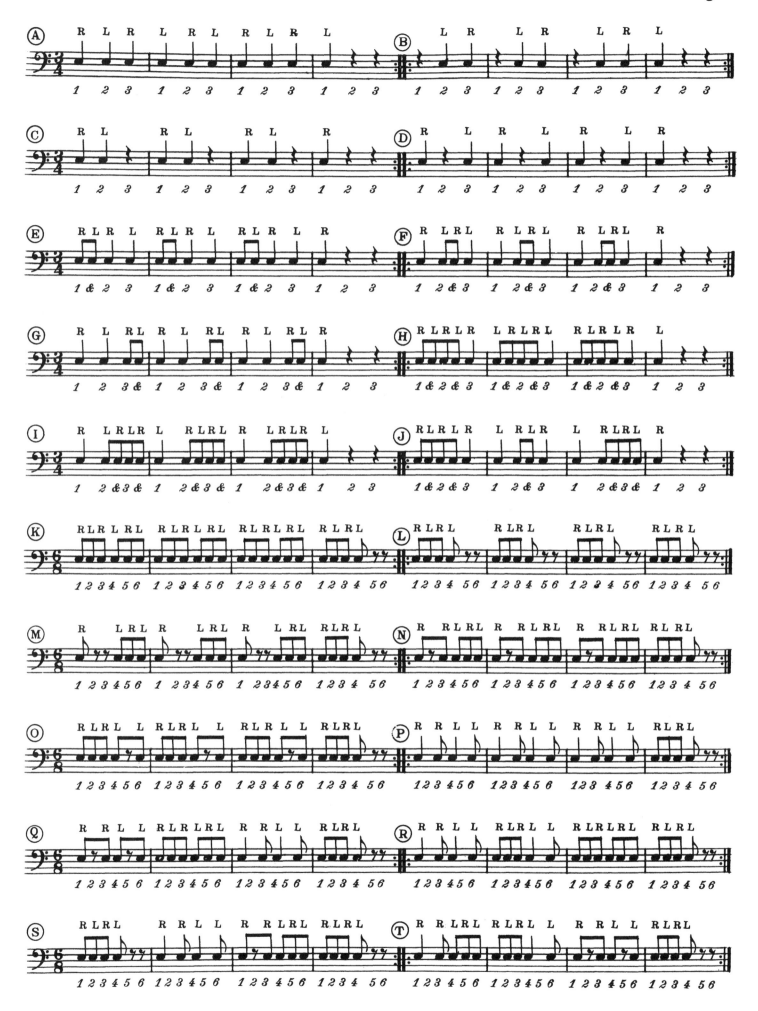

The Five Stroke Roll

The Five Stroke Roll is played in this manner, beginning and ending with the same stick but may be started from either hand.

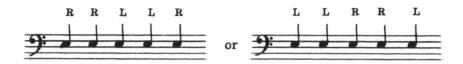

As an exercise, this roll should be started very slowly and gradually speeded up to the limit of the per - former's ability and then just as gradually slowed down to the starting point. In ordinary march tempo the Five Stroke Roll would be written as follows:

Five Stroke Roll as written

If the tempo were slower than that of a march these rolls would necessarily contain more than five strokes and the number of strokes would depend entirely upon the tempo taken and upon the ability of the per - former to execute a closed roll.

The Nine Stroke Roll

The Nine Stroke Roll is played in this manner, beginning and ending with the same stick but may be started from either hand.

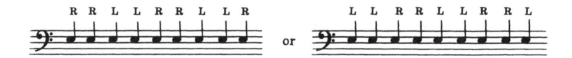

As an exercise, this roll should be started very slowly and gradually speeded up to the limit of the per - former's ability and then just as gradually slowed down to the starting point. In ordinary march tempo the Nine Stroke Roll would be written as follows:

Nine Stroke Roll as written

If the tempo were slower than that of a march these rolls would necessarily contain more than nine strokes and the number of strokes would depend entirely upon the tempo taken and upon the ability of the per - former to execute a closed roll.

Studies for Snare Drum

Introducing the Five and Nine Stroke Rolls.

(5 Stroke Roll)

(9 Stroke Roll)

(9 Stroke Roll)

Dotted Notes

A dot placed after a note increases the value of that note by one half its original value.

Thus a half note ♩ ordinarily equal in time value to two quarters becomes equal to three quarters when the dot is added ♩.

Therefore in the following figure the time value of the dotted half is three times that of the quarter — the dotted quarter three times that of the eighth — etc.

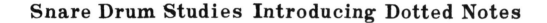

Snare Drum Studies Introducing Dotted Notes

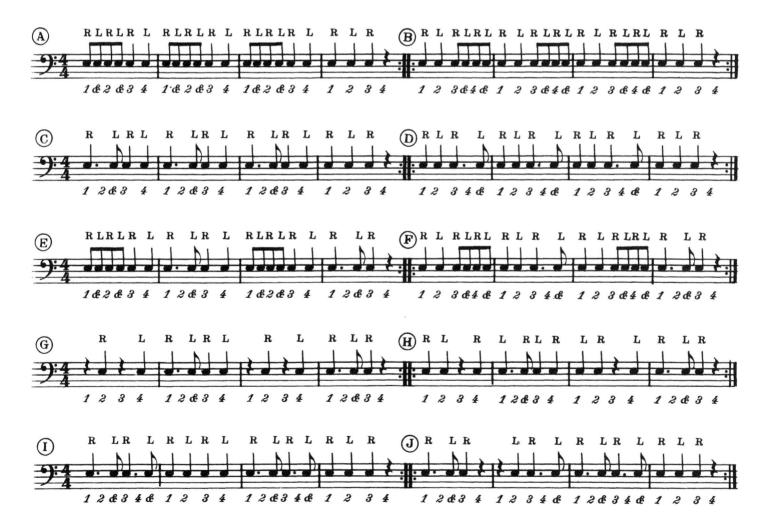

The Flam

The Flam is a grace note played just before the note which follows it and with the opposite stick from that which plays the large note. It may be played with either hand.

The Flam is written as follows:

It should sound exactly as the word is pronounced— Flam — the grace note coming just before the large note.

Snare Drum Studies Introducing the Flam

The Seven Stroke Roll

The Seven Stroke Roll is played in this manner and is always started only with the left stick — ending on the right.

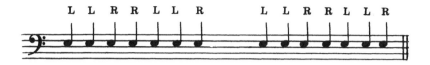

As an exercise it should be started very slowly and gradually speeded up to the limit of the performer's ability then just as gradually slowed down to the starting point.

In ordinary march tempo the Seven Stroke Roll would be written as follows.:

If the tempo were slower than that of a march these rolls would necessarily contain more than seven strokes and the number of strokes would depend entirely upon the tempo taken and the ability of the performer.

Snare Drum Studies

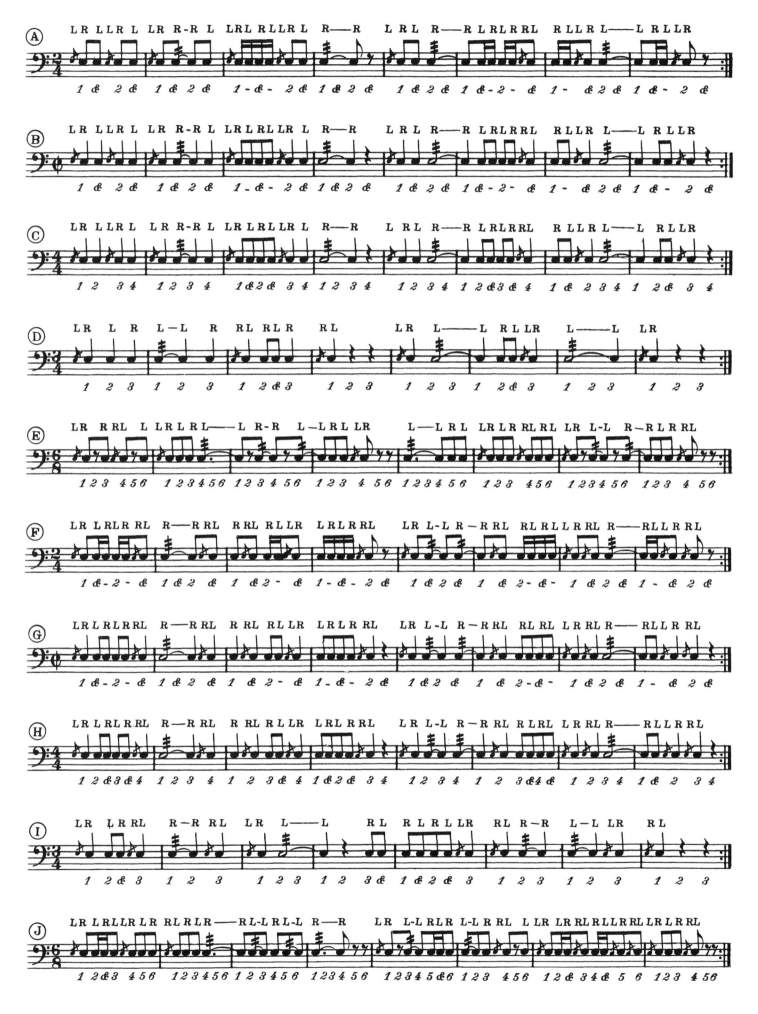

Four Street Beats

ROLL OFF (Signal for band to play)

SHORT ROLL OFF

The Bass Drum

The student at this stage of advancement, in addition to taking up the bass drum, should turn to page 33, and study in a systematic fashion, the famous "twenty-six rudiments" of drumming.

The bass drum is one of the most important instruments in the band or orchestra and should be played by a very capable performer. The drummer must be able to read and should never attempt to "follow along by ear" as is too often the case.

The bass drum should be played with a soft lamb's wool beater in preference to the old hard felt type which does not produce a good tone. For the best tone the drummer should strike the bass drum about half way between the center and the upper hoop. Best results will be obtained from a glancing down and up stroke rather than beating straight into the drum.

At the close of a phrase or strain it is necessary to dampen the bass drum with the free hand so it will not be heard to ring after the other instruments have released their tone.

The roll on the bass drum can be made with a single bass drum beater if it is provided with a small wool ball at the other end of the stick. Two tympani sticks used to execute a single stroke roll on the bass drum will serve better if time is provided in the number for preparing to play this way.

The bass drummer is often called upon to play the cymbals at the same time. In this case one cymbal should be attached to the bass drum with a good holder and the other cymbal hung on a leather thong and held in the left hand of the drummer. The cymbals should not come directly together but the stroke should come a little from the lower side, striking the cymbal when they are exactly even and passing on over the upper side. The use of one performer for both of these instruments serves to give fine precision but will not give the best cymbal tone. For forte or double forte cymbal solos a pair of good cymbals should be struck together by another performer. Many bands use a separate player for cymbals all of the time.

A good bass drummer will learn to memorize four to eight measures of music at a glance and will then keep his eyes riveted on the director to be sure that the tempo does not vary in the least.

Studies for Bass Drum

Studies for Bass and Snare Drum

Cymbals

Introducing some typical cymbal solos as written in drum parts. These are played with a pair of cymbals if available otherwise strike cymbal with a drumstick.

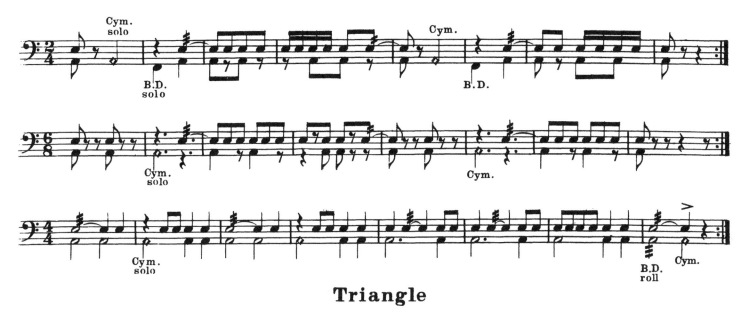

Triangle

The triangle should always be played with a metal beater. The roll is made by rapid strokes of the beater inside one corner of the triangle. Some quick changes from sticks to beater will be necessary in the following parts.

Tom Tom

The Tom Tom or Indian Drum is usually played with one stick alone to give the proper effect. The snare drum with the snares thrown off will serve in absence of a regular Tom Tom.

Castanets and Tambourine

The castanets are usually held in one hand and struck against the other. The tambourine roll is produced either by rapidly shaking the instrument or by running the moistened thumb around the edge of the head.

Wood Block

The wood block is used a great deal for special effects. It is best played with the shank of the sticks about one inch from the top.

The Busy Drummer

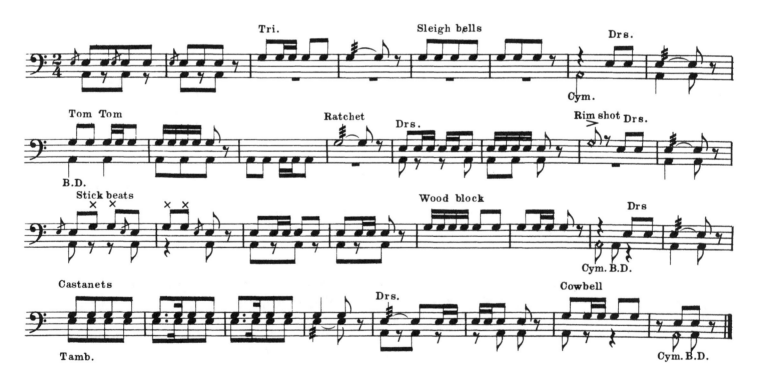

The above part is an example of the various effects a drummer may be called on to produce. Though the changes are not usually as rapid as this the drummer must be able to figure out the part so that all effects may be produced at the proper time. It is often necessary to play one of the above instruments with with one hand while the other is busy preparing the next effect.

The following drum parts are taken from the regular Rubank Band edition and can be had for full Band instrumentation.

Blue Eagle
March

ARTHUR JOHNSON

Star
March

E. De LAMATER

The Old Army Game
Medley of Army Marching Songs

Arr. by PAUL YODER

The Drummers Delight
A Snappy Flashy Drum Novelty

D - bass drum alone
C - cymbal
T - both together
Always both together unless otherwise indicated

STEVE EDWARDS

NOTE: Drummers this is a flashy Jazzy number and Your chance to shine. Pep it up. If you haven't the traps called for, put in something else snappy and step on it.

Tonawanda
Dance of the Indian Camp

A. F. WENDLAND

Southern World
Characteristic Overture

ED CHENETTE

Castanets Tambourine
Small Tom Tom & large
Tom Tom or Chinese Drum

Big Bass Drum

Featuring Drum throughout with Song and Bass Drum Solos in the Trio.

PAUL YODER

TRIO

1st time Sn. Dr. all sing.

Just see how he swings on that big bass drum he hits it some B.D. the great big

bum. Just see how he swings when the ac - cents come, he nev-er missed a sin - gle one.

one play others sing

Just see how he swings on that

bass drum on that big bass drum. *all play*

Developing the Twenty-Six Rudiments of Drumming
(The Scales of the Drum)

Repeat each exercise many times; gradually increase the tempo until the desired effect is obtained.

No.1: Long Roll

No.2: Five Stroke Roll

No.3: Seven Stroke Roll

No.4: Flam

No. 5: Flam Accent No. 1

No. 5a: Flam Accent No. 2

No. 6: Flam Paradiddle

No. 7: Flamacue

No. 8: Ruff

No. 8a: Three Stroke Ruff

No. 8b: Four Stroke Ruff

No. 9: Single Drag

No.10: Double Drag

No.11: Double Paradiddle

No.12: Single Ratamacue

No.13: Triple Ratamacue

No.14: Single Stroke Roll

No.15: Nine Stroke Roll

No.16: Ten Stroke Roll

No.17: Eleven Stroke Roll

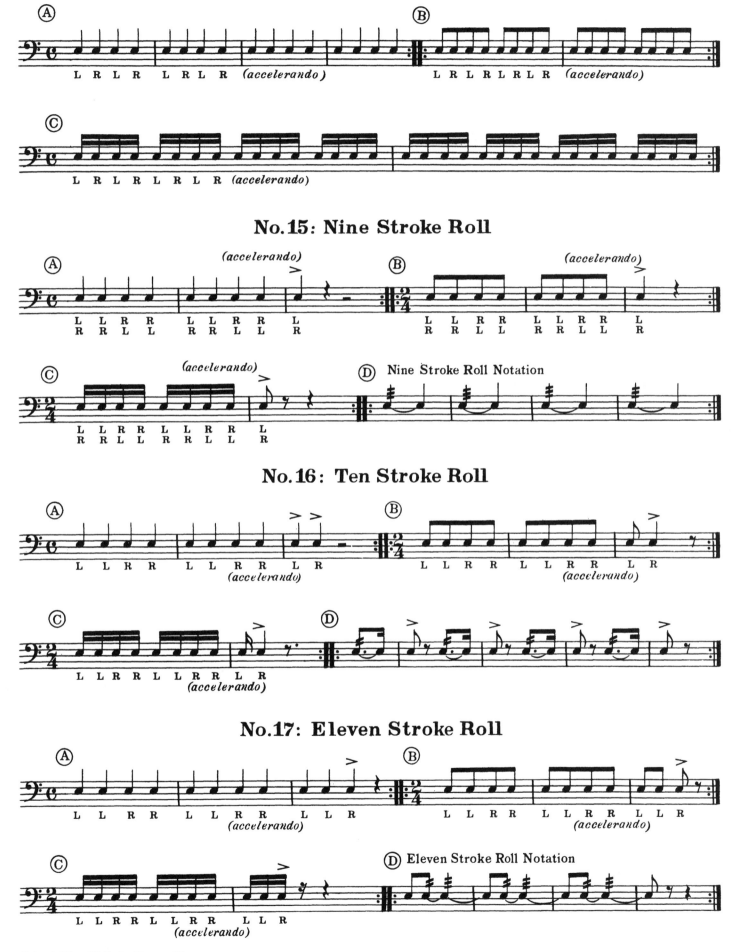

No.18: Thirteen Stroke Roll

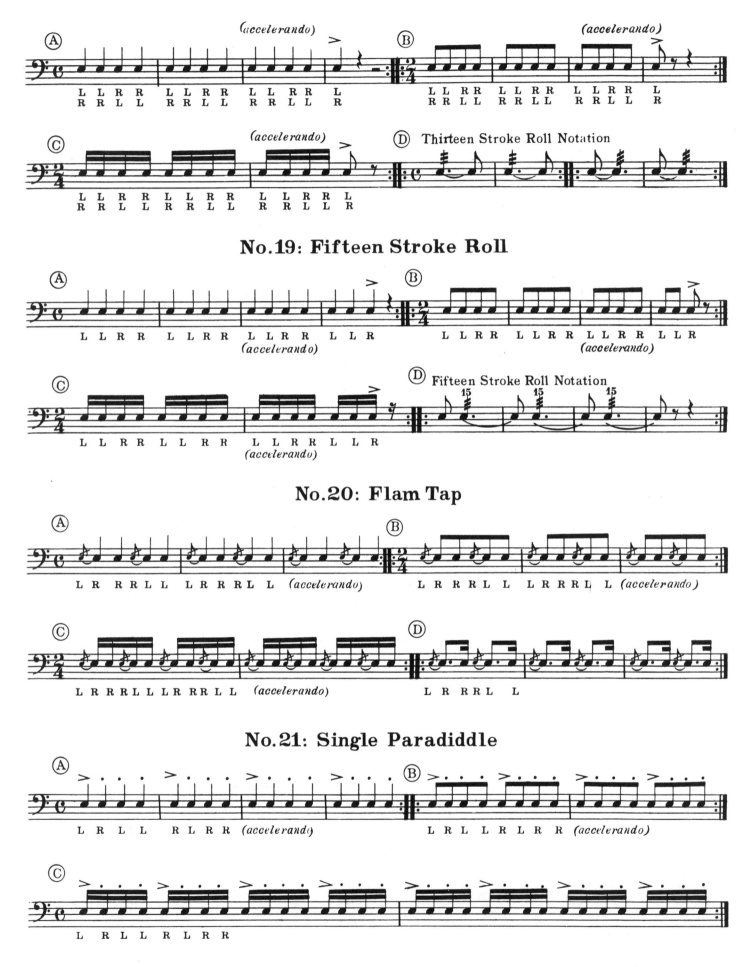

No.19: Fifteen Stroke Roll

No.20: Flam Tap

No.21: Single Paradiddle

No. 21a: Triple Paradiddle

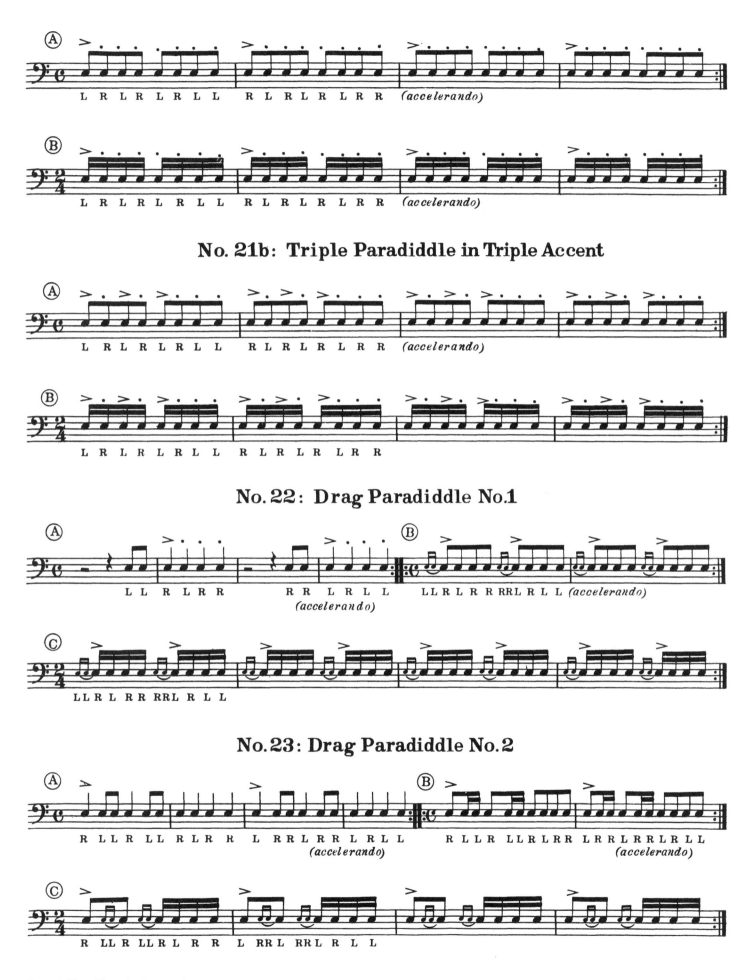

No. 21b: Triple Paradiddle in Triple Accent

No. 22: Drag Paradiddle No.1

No. 23: Drag Paradiddle No.2

No. 24: Flam Paradiddle-Diddle

No. 25: Ratatap*

No. 26: Double Ratamacue

* Commonly know as "Lesson No. 25," this rudiment has been designated "The Ratatap" by the eminent drum authority, William F. Ludwig.